SNAP SHOT™

Senior Editor Mary Ling
Art Editor Joanna Pocock
Editor Finbar Hawkins
Designer Claire Penny
Production Catherine Semark

A SNAPSHOT™ BOOK

SNAPSHOT™ is an imprint of Covent Garden Books.
95 Madison Avenue
New York, NY 10016

Every effort has been made
to trace the copyright holders and we
apologize in advance for any unintentional
omissions. We would be pleased to
insert the appropriate acknowledgment
in any subsequent edition
of this publication.

ISBN 1-56458-734-7
Color reproduction by Colourscan
Printed and bound in Belgium by Proost

On the Farm

Contents

Waiting to hatch

This mother hen is sitting
on a nest of new eggs.
Her feathers keep
the eggs warm
and safe until
they hatch
into chicks.

Ruling the roost

This rooster guards
the hens and shows
off his bright tail.
He wakes everyone
in the mornings with a loud
"Cock-a-doodle-do!"

Counting eggs

How many eggs
can you see?

Where's Mom gone?

Eggs hatch into chirping chicks.
Their down is very soft and
fluffy, but will soon be covered
with feathers. These chicks are
on the lookout for their mom.

Can I go out to play,

nanny?

A nanny goat watches her kid. It has grown horns, and wants to butt with the other goats. Don't try this – unless you have horns, too!

What's for lunch, pigs?

Two little pigs are fed by the farmer.
They are always hungry, and love to
chomp. These piglets will grow up
to be big pigs, just like their dad.

Which way to the water?

These ducks are waddling down to the stream. Mother duck is going to teach her ducklings how to find food.

Hissssss!
Hisssssss!

Geese make good
guards. They can scare off
strangers with a fierce "hiss!"

Did you whistle?

This dog helps a farmer herd flocks of sheep into pens and fields. A sheepdog listens carefully to its master's whistles. On wrong move, and all the sheep will scatter!

Milk is good for

me and you!

A cow makes milk to feed her calf.
The calf needs this milk to help it grow.
There are lots of good things in milk
that help people grow, too!

Crunch, crunch!

A foal tests its teeth on some tasty apples.
Soon it will have strong teeth and jaws,
like its parents. Keep crunching, little pony!

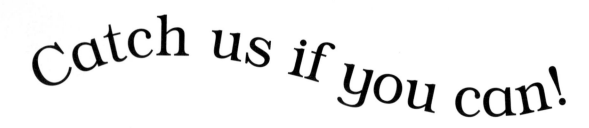

Catch us if you can!

Hungry mice like to nibble the farmer's grain. Only one thing frightens them away, and that's the farmer's cat! Eeek!

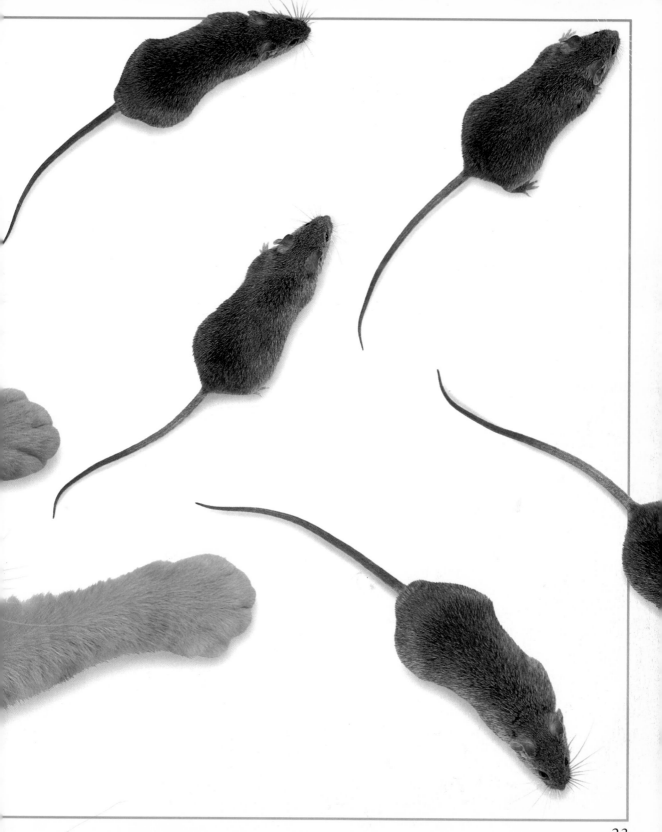

What does

The farmer gathers his crops with a combine harvester. A combine makes about 1,000 cuts a minute – like a huge lawn mower!

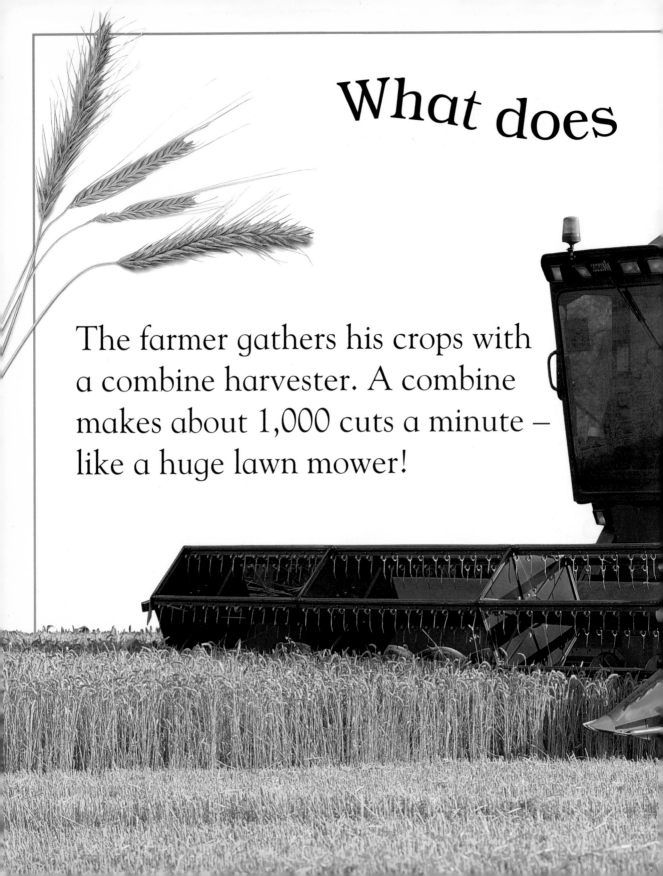

this machine do?

Tractors work all

year round.

A tractor is a very useful vehicle. It can plow fields, mow grass, or carry hay bales. Its big wheels can trundle easily over the muddiest ground.

The super
speedy seed sower!

Once the farmer has plowed the earth, he attaches a machine called a seed drill to his tractor. Then he drives to and fro across the fields, laying seeds in the fresh soil.

Can you name

the babies?

These animal babies are heading back to the farm. Can you name them?

Answers on page 32

Answers

Piglet
Foal
Calf
Duckling
Chick